Sharde,

May God bless :)
for all your genuine love
and compassion for young people.
You are truly an inspiration.
Continue to strive for excellence
and greatness. May God bless
you with love and life.

A Heart to Give
A Journal of Transformation

Adam Harris

iUniverse, Inc.
New York   Bloomington

A Heart to Give
A Journal of Transformation

Copyright © 2010 by Adam Harris

Cover Photograph by David Kimmel

All rights reserved. No part of this book may be used or reproduced by any means, graphic, electronic, or mechanical, including photocopying, recording, taping or by any information storage retrieval system without the written permission of the publisher except in the case of brief quotations embodied in critical articles and reviews.

iUniverse books may be ordered through booksellers or by contacting:

iUniverse
1663 Liberty Drive
Bloomington, IN 47403
www.iuniverse.com
1-800-Authors (1-800-288-4677)

Because of the dynamic nature of the Internet, any Web addresses or links contained in this book may have changed since publication and may no longer be valid. The views expressed in this work are solely those of the author and do not necessarily reflect the views of the publisher, and the publisher hereby disclaims any responsibility for them.

ISBN: 978-1-4502-3014-8 (sc)
ISBN: 978-1-4502-3015-5 (ebook)

Library of Congress Control Number: 2010906301

Printed in the United States of America

iUniverse rev. date: 06/08/2010

Contents

Acknowledgements		vii
The Good Samaritan		xi
Preface		xv
Chapter 1	Before the Journey	1
Chapter 2	The Journey	9
Chapter 3	After the Journey	23
Chapter 4	My Empowerment	27
Chapter 5	A Friend's Perspective	33
Chapter 6	What did I learn?	39
Chapter 7	How you can get Involved	47
The Ultimate Goal		55
A True Heart to Give: Gloria House		57
About the Author		61
My Prayer Today		67

Acknowledgements

I must give honor to God, who allowed me to live in this moment in time where change is on the rise and people are not as resistant to change as in earlier generations. His presence in my life has been the drive of my purpose, the light of my faith and the will of my testimony. I am happy to share my life with Him, and to Him I give the honor, glory and praise.

I deeply thank my mother for giving me the inspiration to write a book about my journey of service and community engagement within the Gulf Coast region of Southwest Louisiana. After a trip to New Orleans, Louisiana, my mom surprised me with a question that I will never forget. She said: "Son, how does it feel to be a leader?" I wasn't quite sure how to respond because I never knew that my mom looked at me as a leader, neither did I feel that she regarded my actions and behaviors as examples of leadership.

When I think of my Mom, I cherish the mother to son relationship that we have. She is always there to give me support and advice when I need it, and she stays on me like a really tough coach. I say a tough coach because if she needed me to write something down and I didn't have a pen at that moment she would say, "Adam, you can never become a good business man until you learn to have a pen with you at all times." Sometimes

I would feel bothered by the very fact that she would challenge my entire future and career as a failure unless I had a pen at that moment. I was going to school for Business Administration, and she made sure to test me on my business etiquette at home. However, I have learned to keep a pen with me at all times, and I know that she just wants me to be the best that I can be.

I also give much gratitude and acknowledgement to my late father, Allen B. Harris. There is not one day that passes that I don't think about him and the significant role he played in my life. Even though he was only alive to see me enter middle school, those eleven years with him gave me much wisdom and knowledge about life and how to handle different situations. He led by example and because I am the youngest of his 12 children, I work every day to make him proud of me by carrying on his great legacy of serving others in the surrounding community.

I would like to thank my family, friends and inner support group that continues to be the foundation of everything that I do. All the things I am a part of could not be possible without these people. So many students, staff and faculty at the University of Michigan-Dearborn played a part in me becoming the young man that I am today that I cannot say thank you enough. I tend to surround myself with very positive people who are of different races, creeds, religious affiliations, and beliefs. To me it doesn't really matter who you are or what your background is; but it does matter where you're headed and whether you have a positive outlook on life. I quote my mom and an old cliché that says, "If you are not a part of the solution, then you may be a part of the problem." Sometimes we can be blinded by our own outlook on life and not see the answers to some of our own problems because we won't listen to someone who does not look like us (on the outside). However, if we as human beings could see past a person's skin color, or ascribed status, then we might be able to solve the very problems that our world faces today.

A great deal of gratitude goes out to the many students who were a part of this experience in Lake Charles, Louisiana. What an amazing experience! To meet college students from all over the country who had an understanding of service and the importance of not passing the people of the Gulf Coast region by, reminds me of the story in the Bible of the Good Samaritan. So many of these students could have used this time to enjoy their college spring break, but they chose to lend a helping hand to many people in need. God bless you for your time and service to the region of Southwest Louisiana.

Lastly, a special thank you goes to United Way for giving me the opportunity to volunteer in the Alternative Spring Break Program. This experience could not have been possible without their support, funding and belief in local college students to make a difference. They have changed my life and my outlook on life for the better, and I greatly appreciate it. May God Bless you also!

The Good Samaritan
Luke 10:25-37

25 And, behold, a certain lawyer stood up, and tempted him, saying, Master, what shall I do to inherit eternal life? **26** He said unto him, WHAT IS WRITTEN IN THE LAW? HOW READEST THOU? **27** And he answering said, Thou shalt love the Lord thy God with all thy heart, and with all thy soul, and with all thy strength, and with all thy mind; and THY NEIGHBOUR AS THYSELF. **28** And he said unto him, THOU HAST ANSWERED RIGHT: THIS DO, AND THOU SHALT LIVE. **29** But he, willing to justify himself, said unto Jesus, And who is my neighbor?
30 And Jesus answering said, A CERTAIN MAN WENT DOWN FROM JERUSALEM TO JERICHO, AND FELL AMONG THIEVES, WHICH STRIPPED HIM OF HIS RAINMENT, AND WOUNDED HIM, AND DEPARTED, LEAVING HIM HALF DEAD. **31** AND BY CHANCE THERE CAME DOWN A CERTAIN PRIEST THAT WAY: AND WHEN HE SAW HIM, HE PASSED BY ON THE OTHER SIDE. **32** AND LIKEWISE A LEVITE, WHEN HE WAS AT THE PLACE, CAME AND LOOKED ON HIM, AND PASSED BY ON THE OTHER SIDE. **33** BUT A CERTAIN SAMARITAN, AS HE JOURNEYED, CAME WHERE HE

WAS: AND WHEN HE SAW HIM, HE HAD COMPASSION ON HIM, **34** AND WENT TO HIM, AND BOUND UP HIS WOUNDS, POURING IN OIL AND WINE, AND SET HIM ON HIS OWN BEAST, AND BROUGHT HIM TO AN INN, AND TOOK CARE OF HIM. **35** AND ON THE MORROW WHEN HE DEPARTED, HE TOOK OUT TWO PENCE, AND GAVE THEM TO THE HOST, AND SAID UNTO HIM, TAKE CARE OF HIM; AND WHATSOEVER THOU SPENDEST MORE, WHEN I COME AGAIN, I WILL REPAY THEE. **36** WHICH NOW OF THESE THREE, THINKEST THOU, WAS NEIGHBOUR UNTO HIM THAT FELL AMONG THE THIEVES?

37 And he said, He that shewed mercy on him. Then said Jesus unto him, GO AND DO THOU LIKEWISE.

KING JAMES VERSION (KJV)

What do you need to serve?

Find your answer inside **A Heart to Give***...*

Preface

Living is the art of loving. Loving is the art of caring. Caring is the art of sharing. Sharing is the art of living. If you want to lift yourself up, lift up someone else.

—Booker T. Washington

There comes a time in our lives where we begin to look beyond ourselves to truly appreciate the value of others. Depending on whom you are this realization and new perspective on life can socially learned or forced upon you in a moment to under the inequity of our society itself. Sometimes it's as if bulb turns on and you finally realize that you don't live alone or by yourself, but you can turn to others for h the one lending a helping hand. At that moment yo value the collectivistic nature of our society that all interdependent upon one another. It seems to lie America values as the individual. In fact Dr. Mar Jr. says, "An individual has not started living above the narrow confines of his individualis broader concerns of all humanity."

It was my junior year and I was well ir the University of Michigan-Dearborn. I classes, working part time and playing basketball for the university as well. I didn't have much of a social life because between basketball, school and work, that took up quite a bit of my time during daylight hours. Just before midterms and Thanksgiving break which was vastly approaching, I learned about a trip that I could take called "Alternative Spring Break".

Now I must admit Spring Break to college students is like the ultimate time off from school. It can be portrayed as the utopian college vacation and time away to have fun. To the typical college student, one begins to think of the beaches along the coast of Florida or finding a place to get away with friends. It brings so much excitement and hype that students cannot help themselves to ask others, "Where are you going for Spring Break?" And this thinking process begins way before the New Year marches in.

One day as I was walking through the University Center on campus which is central to all campus life at our university, I happened to walk into my friend that I had met over the summer at a joint. She began to explain to me how she was planning to take this Alternative Spring Break trip to help rebuild houses from the devastation of Hurricane Rita. She told me it was a week of service in the Gulf Coast Region and the group was taking care of all the expenses for the trip. First, when I heard hearing this idea of being socially responsible as a college student truly shocked me because everything I had thought when I felt Break before that moment was contrary to what you would do for preserving Mother Nature. Secondly, when I heard I didn't have to pay a dime, I was all in. Say what you can truly say about nothing being free in America, but I knew that We were going to have this trip and it was not coming out of my pocket.

The Way was sponsoring us for this experience because United Way felt and they wanted to know about each individual who was planning on participating in this week of service in the Gulf coast. It was also their way to show the consciousness of young adults in college and our will to give back to an area recovering from a disaster. Well it was about a week later, when I decided to apply online for this experience and I was very impatient about the long process.

Finally, one day, I received an email after waiting a few months that said that I would be able to participate in United Way's Alternative Spring Break Program in Lake Charles, Louisiana. From there I was excited and could finally move on with my life from waiting many days and weeks for a confirmation to participate in the experience. I wrote about my feelings, ideas and thoughts about this process and experience with United Way and I have put them within the pages of this book.

A Heart to Give chronicles my thoughts before, during and after Alternative Spring Break 2007 in Lake Charles, Louisiana. This experience came right after my participation in a long and very tiring basketball season at the University of Michigan-Dearborn. This trip would be my first adventure outside the state of Michigan by myself, and without my family. It would also be my first time on an airplane, an up close and personal look at the devastation of Hurricane Rita, and an opportunity for me and other students at the University to meet and greet each other; as well as meeting other students from around the country.

The Alternative Spring Break Program is a week long service event that immerses college students from around the country in an experience to rebuild hurricane devastated areas and inner-city communities around the country. However the week of service does not involve just community service, but it also allows the students after each day to learn and reflect about the community in which they are serving. This experience was coordinated by United

Way of America; however, our local United Way for Southeastern Michigan did a great job with getting all the Michigan students the necessary information that we needed to participate in this week of service near the Gulf coast.

Going into the experience, I did not know what to expect; however, I did know that I wanted to help the area of southwest Louisiana as much as I possibly could. Randy Dillard, who now serves as the Director of Volunteer Services at United Way for Southeastern Michigan, was the Student Activities Supervisor at University of Michigan-Dearborn at the time. He was very instrumental in connecting students from University of Michigan-Dearborn to this life-changing experience.

As you read through my journals within this book, you will be able to place yourself in my shoes and be there with me every step of the way. You will be able to learn about me as a person, and about the transformative experience I had that made me begin to look at problems around the country on a macro level. Hurricane Rita was a category 3 hurricane that made landfall in 2005. Experts say that Rita caused 11.3 billion dollars in damage, and was recorded as the fourth-most intense Atlantic hurricane (wikipedia.org). As I read about the devastation that Rita caused along the Gulf coast area, it really motivated me to make a conscious decision to make the trip to Southwest Louisiana.

When I got home from the experience, I began to write even more about how thankful I was to United Way for providing me with such a transformative experience. I would like to point out that the turning point and transformative moment for me was during the phone conversation that I had with my Mom. It was during the last day of my experience, and she gave me words of encouragement, while also giving me a sense of responsibility at my lowest moment. That sense of responsibility was that I would come back and be more involved in my community locally, here in Southeastern Michigan.

To learn more about the United Way Alternative Spring Break Program please visit: *http://www.liveunited.org/asb.*

I entitled this book *A Heart to Give* because it truly expresses the passion that I have to give back to the community through volunteer efforts and being of service to others. I have always cared for my community, and those who are unfortunate to help themselves, but after this experience it was as if a light bulb turned on inside of me. I am quite sure that my family, including my peers, did not expect that this trip would bring such a transformation to my life but it was unexpected for me as well. However, I am grateful and thankful to not only the experience but to all the college students who gave up their Spring Break to help the area of Southwest Louisiana.

I am very thankful to have this opportunity to share my story with you. Writing this book allows me to bring my Alternative Spring Break experience full circle. In some of my journals before the experience, I explain about my passion to give back and I also give a bit of information about who I am as a person. This passion of community involvement has been a part of me ever since I was a little child. Having that sense of compassion and empathy for my community was always deeply rooted in my values, and my journals will begin to show you how important service to the community is to me.

Adam Harris
Southfield, MI
August 2008

1
Before the Journey

The best way to find yourself, is to loose yourself in the service of others.
—Mahatma Gandhi

In this chapter you will get to know a little about me as a person before the Alternative Spring Break experience. The journals that are in this chapter were my notes before my experience in Lake Charles, Louisiana. These journals were also responses to questions that United Way for Southeastern Michigan sent to the local Michigan participants of Alternative Spring Break 2007, so that they could learn about who the participants were as people and our passion to give back. It is my hope that you can see that my passion for community involvement started before this experience, and is very close to my heart as our nation continues to battle many domestic and global issues.

Friday, February 9, 2007
Introduction

I am 20 years old. I'm in my third year at the University of Michigan-Dearborn. I play on the Men's Varsity Basketball Team and I'm also affiliated with other organizations. My major is Business Management and Supply Chain Management, with a minor in African and African American Studies. I am very proud and thankful to be here and grateful to have this opportunity.

I applied for Alternative Spring Break (ASB) because I saw an opportunity to deeply enrich myself in service by helping others. As we look around, there are many things that we take for granted that might be here today and gone tomorrow. I realized that I have been blessed all my life with health, strength, shelter, food and clothing. Now is the time that I can lend a helping hand to comfort another individual who might be living in despair.

Choosing ASB 2007 was not a question for me, but more of an answer. During the year, I have very little time to spend hanging out because of basketball and school, so I would use every opportunity to be with my family or involved in an activity that would make me a better humanitarian.

From this experience, I hope to gain a sense of contribution to my society. We tend to live life in an individualistic comfort zone, not realizing that others can use our help, whether it would be a kind word, a helping hand or just a smile to brighten someone else's day. I am very thankful to be a participant of ASB 2007.

Friday, February 9, 2007
Why I applied

I first heard about Alternative Spring Break from a friend of mine who was interested in going but couldn't go because of other reasons. When I first heard about it and I read the flyer, I thought it was too good to be true to have a paid trip to help out individuals in Louisiana suffering from tragic despair. Talking with Randy Dillard, who is a staff member in the Student Activities Office at the University of Michigan-Dearborn, he reassured me that this was "the real deal." After the reassurance, I only needed to check my basketball schedule to see if there would be a time conflict between the two events. I was happy to find out that my basketball season would be done by this point and that I would be able to go. I LOVE basketball so don't think I'm happy to see the end of the season.

I see this event as a great opportunity for me to continue my involvement in community service. This time it gives me a chance to step outside the box and see how a single event can change the lives of individuals physically, psychologically, and socially. If I'm able to help take out trash or help put up a wall or to even show a smile to allow individuals to be relieved from their current situation (even for a second), I will feel that I've made a contribution. My parents have always encouraged me to stay involved and to lend a helping hand in my community. So I look forward to the challenge, the opportunity and experience of ASB 2007. "Many hands make light work" (grandmother), so I look forward to being a part of this team in making this project lighter.

Saturday February 10, 2007
My Reaction

My reaction when I found out I was accepted to ASB...

I was reading my email one day and I saw an email sent from United Way of Southeastern Michigan. The email read: "Good afternoon, you have been chosen to be a participant in United Way for Southeastern Michigan's Alternative Spring Break 2007 in partnership with thinkMTV and United Way of America." I wasn't quite sure what I had done or why I was chosen because we had to apply before Christmas break and I had forgotten all about it.

Many emotional thoughts began to hit me at once because I understood that I would be helping individuals in a society dealing with a crisis that had caused many lives to be lost, and much pain and emotional strife. A person's entire life orientation can be changed by a crisis such as this.

As I began to thank God for the opportunity, I realized that this event would continue to help me become the holistic person I strive to be. It brings back memories of my father and the stories that he told me about working along side Rev. Jesse Jackson. Being involved in the Patty Hearst capture, my father said he helped feed thousands of people, and also prayed for individuals in need. Having lost my father to a heart attack and stroke in 1998, I take pride in being a part of his legacy of hard work. His death has kept me close to my roots and true to my values and morals.

Alternative Spring Break will also contribute to my minor in African and African American Studies. Many of my classes under my minor degree are cross-listed with sociology, so an understanding of how individuals interact with each other when they are subjected to devastating environmental conditions is essential to this experience. I am very thankful to the person who read my application because they have given me a chance to show my volunteer efforts on a national stage. Even though I will be missing a full week of school, I realize I will be gaining a full week of hands-on education. So I look forward to working with many individuals from all over the country. With many of the team members sharing the same desire to help out, I feel that I will be a part of a team that has succeeded even before the mission is carried out.

Friday, February 23, 2007
My Expectations

I am really excited and looking forward to meeting the individuals from all over the country who have committed themselves to this experience. As we close in on the last couple of days before our trip, I am very anxious to experience my first commercial airline flight. What a feeling of excitement!

I look forward to meeting the faces and people behind this tragedy because I'm sure their lives will never be the same. The beauty of this experience is that everyone has come together in unison to say, "I've been blessed during my life; so let me bless another person."

I also look forward to the hard manual labor that is needed. I'm sure debris must be removed, walls will need reconstruction and homes will need to be rebuilt. So as the days and moments continue to count down, I pray that God will bless us on this trip and bless the individuals that have experienced the loss of their homes and valuables.

Friday, March 2, 2007
What I Am Most and Least Excited About

We are officially one week away and the momentum of excitement continues to build. Each day I find myself talking more and more to my colleagues who are joining me on this trip. Randy, who is a staff member at the University of Michigan-Dearborn, is really trying to keep his cool because he leaves on Wednesday, March 7th. I am really excited and can't wait.

On the other hand I am least excited about missing an entire week of school. This week has been very strange because I have been on campus everyday studying even though this week was my university's Spring Break. Also I will be missing my Mom and family whom I love so dearly.

Friday, March 9, 2007
My Thoughts on Hurricane Katrina

I remember following the news everyday when New Orleans and other states were undergoing the devastating hurricanes. Every night I would pray for the individuals who didn't leave their homes in time or weren't able to leave to escape the tragic weather. Following the sources of media very closely, I couldn't begin to even imagine myself in such a position. Families lost their loved ones, homes, valuables, and their entire community. The one story from the news that hit me the most was reported by Robin Roberts. She shared her personal connection to the tragedy. I began to feel her pain, when I realized that this is a situation that people had no control over.

So it means a lot to me to have this opportunity right before me. As we continue to battle problems all over the world, we are still fighting the battle of post Katrina. My heart goes out to every individual affected by the hurricane. That includes the families directly affected and the families who had to respond to the needs of their extended family. I hope that my individual effort can help give comfort to let the individuals of Louisiana know that there are still people who care about them very much. God bless you, and I will be in Lake Charles tomorrow.

2
The Journey

Never doubt that a small group of thoughtful committed citizens can change the world; indeed, it's the only thing that ever has.

–**Margaret Mead**

My journals in this chapter portray my service in the field each day with my team that I was assigned to for the week. However what the journals seem to leave out are the moments in the evening, at the housing center after our day of service in the area. I mentioned that this experience was comprised of students from across the country, who represented a variety of colleges, universities and communities. The beauty of knowing this was trying to meet as many students as possible, to expand your network and friendship across the country.

In my generation (Millennials), we are hooked to this new social network called Facebook. I remember staying up late nights talking with students, while some students were playing cards, watching March Madness or in the gym shooting basketballs. As I would conclude my conversation with another student, there was always one question that seemed to come up, "Are you on Facebook?" This was a concern for me at the time because I had problems joining the new internet based social network because I felt that our society was being divided by it. I was raised in a very traditional family and I remember having my first cell phone at the age of 18. However it seems that our society is growing so rapidly today that students in elementary school have cell phones now.

My bias against this new wave of technology turned around and slapped me in the face. I was probably the only person asking other students to write their name and number on a piece of paper that was provided at the housing center. I was old school and because of this experience, I finally joined Facebook and added all the people that I met as friends. Some times you just have to go with the current and not against it.

The beauty of meeting so many students from across the country was the camaraderie and excitement we shared after the experience. For myself, I remembered seeing tons of pictures from the experience that allowed me to reminisce on the time I shared with the other students. I also remember students beginning to post messages on other students Facebook walls about a possible ASB 2007 Reunion. I also recall students bragging about how far their college team went during March Madness. Lastly, some students made such a special bond with others that students were making trips to meet up with their new found friends in other states.

My special moment came when I was told that a young lady that I met at ASB played soccer for University of Southern California. Following the ASB experience, USC was scheduled to play University of Michigan during the upcoming season in Ann Arbor. Well I attended University of Michigan-Dearborn, and I decided to make the trip out to see the game. Not knowing much about soccer, I spoke with Lauren Brown after she beat my school, in what seemed to me to be an easy victory. Later on that year, I found out that USC had won the NCAA Championship in Women's soccer. What a small world to know that I shared the same experience with one of the girls on the team. I was very excited for her and I made sure to congratulate her on the accomplishment.

So as you can see this experience in Louisiana was more than just service. The people that I have met will never be forgotten because there are many pictures, articles and Facebook groups to remind us of the time we shared. I believe that no one can ever measure the impact that this experience had because it takes special people to care about others, and it takes even wonderful people to help others in their time of need.

In this chapter, I will share with you my thoughts about my experience in Lake Charles, Louisiana. In the Preface, I mentioned that this experience would involve my first airplane flight and meeting students from the University of Michigan-Dearborn whom I've never met before. You will find moments when I'm happy, sad, joyful, glad, prayful, thankful, humble and excited. You will relive my experience each day, working with a team of young individuals from all over the country to help rebuild a lady's home that was badly damaged by the hurricane. This experience made me very humble to see that this misfortune can happen anywhere at any time.

Saturday, March 10, 2007
My First Day on the Ground

I'm on the ground and I am very thankful. My first plane ride was great and I had a lot of fun. It was all I expected it to be. As we landed in Houston, Texas, we were greeted by a team of United Way members in the airport. Everyone checked in and received their bags. From the airport we took a van to Lake Charles, Louisiana. The trip took about two hours and we were delayed by a traffic jam. A lot of bonding took place amongst the "Michiganders" in the van.

As we arrived at the Volunteer housing center, we were greeted by many members of United Way. Our photo was taken immediately as we exited the van. Actually, if you check the national United Way website you will see our pictures (we are in red t-shirts). We were given a tour of the housing center and photos of us were taken for every step we made (we began to feel like celebrities). At this moment, I am just enjoying the cool weather that Louisiana is providing for me. Thank you to everyone who sent out prayers for our safe flight down.

Sunday, March 11, 2007
Day Two in Louisiana

Wow! There are over 150 students here from all over the country. I have met people from New Jersey, Texas, Washington, New York, Ohio, Florida and Mississippi. Everyone is so down to earth and very eager to start helping the victims of Louisiana. We also found out today that journalists from all over the world will be writing articles on our experience. I personally got a chance to meet one of the journalists from Turkey. She told me that she is traveling all over the world and the United States doing stories. She shared with me her thoughts on the hurricanes and the devastation of the Gulf coast.

Today we took a tour of the cities affected by Hurricane

Rita. There was total devastation! For miles and miles we looked outside the fifteen passenger van, at land still flooded with water. We saw alligators on the banks of the road, houses destroyed and floating in water, and trees turned over. I personally got choked up because this is all we saw. I began to wonder why it is that more help from the government was not forthcoming. As we continued to ride, we saw many slabs of concrete with no structure on top. I began to pray and reflect upon the images I remembered in the media, when the hurricanes first hit. The tour was an eye-opening experience, proving that there is still much work to be done.

Yesterday, we were assigned the groups that we will be working with for the duration of the break. I am one of two men in my group and the rest are women. Unfortunately, there are two women to every man, so for those that can do the math, there are approximately 100 females and 50 males in total (smiles). We did a lot of team bonding in our groups by telling each other about ourselves. My team leader is from Harlem, New York, and she works in the marketing department for VIBE magazine. Her name is Chauncie and she is very funny. She is very energetic and excited about the opportunity. At the moment, we don't know exactly what project we will be working on, but we will find out early in the morning tomorrow.

After the tour, everyone came back to the housing center to have dinner. We were fed meat loaf, salad, green beans, mashed potatoes, and chicken. The food was great and the chef can really cook. Afterwards, we had an ASB dance that was put on by a local band. Everyone was instructed to go and participate. After the dance it was about time for everyone to go to bed. We have a tough day ahead of us, and I am looking forward to working and doing manual labor.

Monday, March 12, 2007
Day Three: First day on site

Today was a great day. We woke up early this morning at 6:30 a.m. and had breakfast. The United Way team leaders want us loaded in the vans at 8 a.m., leaving and headed toward the site.

My team name is "Da Bears." I did not personally want this name, but the ladies ruled me out. My thought of a team name was "The Saints" because that is the name of the pro football team in New Orleans and the name brings a positive mind set. We met a lady today who was affected by Hurricane Rita. She welcomed us in with opened arms and she was very happy that we had chosen her home to restore.

As we took a tour of her home, it was very hard to realize that she was still living there. The floor had massive holes in it, there were windows that were cracked and she was living in conditions that most citizens wouldn't live in. I gave the lady a lot of credit and respect for being strong and stable. She did not allow herself to be a victim of the disaster, but a survivor.

Today our task was to secure fiber glass in the walls for insulation. The project went very quickly because most of the team was working. After we were done in the kitchen, we moved toward the back of the house where there was a lot of damage. The back of the house took more work and effort because there were some walls that needed to be torn down. After we demolished the walls, we then worked on removing the paneling that had no fiber glass between the inside and outside wood. This part was harder than expected because we had to work around the unstable windows that were sitting in the walls with little support. During the process, we saw some type of lizard that had made himself a home in the wall.

During the day, we also got a chance to meet the lady's two sons. The seven-year-old was very excited to have company, but the four-year-old was a little shy. I took the four-year-old outside and had a race with him in the yard. He beat me every time, but others would say he cheated. I also took a picture of him on the top of a tree stomp. He was excited and posed like a celebrity rapper.

Afterwards we had a photo shoot with MTV and the national United Way. I was personally interviewed by the national United Way and the video should be up pretty soon. Today was a great day because I got a chance to play basketball with some of the students. I did my thing and had fun.

Tuesday, March 13, 2007
Day four: Second Day on site

First and foremost I would like to thank my family and friends for their support and prayers during this week. I have been reading the comments from everyone and I miss you all. I will see you next week!

Each day seems to get more interesting. Today started off a little slow for my crew because we did not have the tools, neither the instructions from the inspector to do our job. Tools such as hammers and drills were needed to start putting up the sheet rock in the kitchen.

As we waited, I pulled out my mp3 player and played some classical R&B for the team. Everyone sat around and chatted with "Rocky" as the music played. Roxanne is the name of the homeowner whose house we are working on but she told us to call her Rocky. Finally, the inspector came and we got to work. With very limited space to work in, everyone worked really hard together to put up the sheet rock in the kitchen. The process was a little slow at the beginning, but it picked up as everyone learned how to do the job.

I must give credit to the 13 ladies in my group because they worked so hard and non stop. For myself, I tried to be the energy behind the team by keeping everyone laughing and smiling. My team leader, Chauncie, has her boyfriend coming in town tomorrow, and I have a challenge set up against him in basketball. I'm sure this will be fun.

Everyday it seems like the team gels more closer together. The bond that we have is becoming stronger because we realize how much each person loves to volunteer his/her time. This is our way of giving back and it helps build us individually as well as collectively. I'm so happy to be a part of this experience. It was all I expected it to be and more.

Wednesday, March 14, 2007
Day Five: A talk with David

It was another successful day at work for the crew. The sheet rock around the kitchen was being put up real fast and everyone was determined to finish the kitchen and the second room. As everyone worked very hard, a news reporter from the local area came to report on our work and experience. The reporter decided to interview Rocky (the home owner) and her two sons, David and Gabriel.

After the interview, Gabe and David began to act up and become extremely playful. When it was time to clean up, Rocky used this time to embarrass her two sons in front of the entire team. At first the team didn't quite understand why but later I had to explain to them the reason for this. In the African American community, if you embarrass your parent or act out in front of a group of people, you better expect to receive the equal treatment and a harsh punishment in return. Rocky began to explain to her sons that our crew was friends of hers and to disrespect her in front of her friends is the worst treatment and humiliation that she could receive. After the conversation, I took David outside and explained to him why his mother was so hard on him.

Standing on the porch with the door closed, I remembered the ways in which I was brought up and the individuals who made impressions upon my life. I shared with David what it's like to be a parent, living day to day in the conditions that his Mom lives in. From the first day, I told David a quote from my childhood that I remembered: "Success comes from the heart." This is a very simple quote but so easy to remember and true in meaning. I explained that honoring his mother is not only a role to which he should adhere, but he should want to do this because it is the only request and expectation of a child, given by God. I told him that if he wants to live a long time, he would be respectful and honorable to his mother, and that by doing this, he would become successful. I also explained to him that education is very important and learning about the fundamental principles of life would help him a great deal. Lastly, I told him to be good and be respectful to everyone, no matter what color or ethnicity they might be. When I was done, I embraced him with a big hug and told him, "I love you." He had a big smile upon his face.

I felt it was my duty to step in the place of a big brother and share with him the respect and care that a son like me gives to his community. I told him about my family and my life, which I love so dearly. When I explained to David that doing things from the heart will get you ahead in life, I told him that this is why I am here in Louisiana today because I love to help and give back.

Thursday, March 15, 2007
Day Six: Tearing up the floor

Energy was on my side today. I woke up from a good night's rest and was eager to get on site for work. We finished the last couple of pieces of sheet rock and the next assignment was to tear up the floor for reconstruction. There are two women in the group who have emerged as leaders. Chauncie and Jing Jing can really work and they generate energy to make sure that we are doing our job. They are two very passionate young ladies and they are enjoying every moment of this experience.

Today we got down and dirty. We finished the sheet rock around the kitchen, and then we started to demolish the floor. Tearing up the floor outside the kitchen was harder than I thought. Layers and layers of wood had been laid down over the years and all of it needed to come up. During the day, we experienced a scary moment because one of the ladies fell through the floor while standing on a soft spot. However, we barely noticed it because it happened so fast and then she immediately jumped back up. She began laughing about the whole thing, but I took the matter very seriously. Good thing there is no basement.

After we got done, it was almost time to leave. We sat down and had a chat with Rocky. She told me that she wanted to introduce me to her niece and she showed me a picture of her. She is a very beautiful girl and she has graduated from school already. We also talked about the next day and she told us that she would miss each and every one of us. As she broke into tears, I gave her a hug and told her that she had my number and could call me at anytime.

So as this week comes to a close, I am sure it will be very hard to leave behind me a family that I've made. From day one, Rocky has opened her home to the crew, and I love her for it. I will miss David and Gabriel because I see very bright futures ahead of them. I just pray that God continues to shelter their family with love and grace and they continue their strength in the Lord.

Friday, March 16, 2007
Emotions Begin to Run

Today was the last official day of Alternative Spring Break 2007. Even though everyone is scheduled to fly out and return to their homes tomorrow, our work is finished today. I found my energy level to be medium today because I was excited about the week I had experienced, but I was saddened that today could be the last time that I might see Rocky and her two sons. Also I will miss all the participants of the event. I pray that everyone has a safe trip home.

What an experience! I feel I have become a better individual and citizen in society. From the tour of Louisiana, to the dormitory experience at the volunteer housing center and the opportunity to help a family in need, I feel that I have evolved into a better human being. At the end of the week-long service project, you walk away feeling high in self-esteem and value to society. You begin to realize that you have taken time out to think about other people who might be less fortunate than yourself.

As I look back upon ASB 2007, I am thankful to all the people and sponsors that made this event possible. First, I must thank United Way of Southeastern Michigan, United Way of America and United Way of Southwest Louisiana. Other sponsors such as FedEx, EB Games, and Nike made this experience one memory that will not be forgotten. Also I must give thanks to Randy, a staff member at the University of Michigan-Dearborn, who made it easier for the students to participate. Also I would like to thank Kawthar that arranged the airline flights and trips to and from the airport. Lastly, I must thank my family, which has supported me every step of the way. I kept in touch with them throughout the week and they have done the same.

As lunchtime began, everyone went out to eat except me, a couple of the girls and Rocky. Rocky could tell I wasn't in full spirits, so she asked me what bothered me. I told her that it was beginning to hit me that today was the last day of ASB and that I would miss the boys and the entire experience. She understood my feelings and told me to call home. I listened and called my Mom. When Rocky talked to her, she told my Mom about my low spirits and how they affected my actions. My mom explained to me that this is a part of life. When you involve yourself in experiences such as this you get attached really quickly and become saddened at the end. The truth is that this will not be the end, but the beginning of the evolution process. It would be the start of a long-term relationship with Rocky and her two sons because I am now a member of their family. I have begun a mentor responsibility with David and Gabriel, so they can call me at anytime about anything. This is also the beginning of doing big things and dreaming that nothing is too hard or impossible to achieve. I feel blessed and delighted that I was chosen for this event.

So as we left, I prayed that Rocky and her family would continue to receive help for the reconstruction of their home. I prayed that David and Gabriel would not be sucked into the world winds of life that oppress people all over the world. I also asked that God would bless the entire state of Louisiana and all the victims of hurricanes Katrina and Rita.

Saturday, March 17, 2007
Words can't even say thank you

Over this past week I've enjoyed an experience that I will never forget and to all the people involved, I would like to say thank you. To United Way of America, I would like to say thanks for setting up an opportunity for young individuals in college to show themselves on a national stage doing volunteer work in the community. To United Way of Southwest Louisiana, I want to thank you for housing all the volunteers from all over the entire country and showing great hospitality to everyone. Also to United Way of Southeastern Michigan, I must thank all the people who worked very hard to make sure that Michigan was represented by ten great individuals. My life has been changed and because of this event, I can go back to my community and volunteer from this experience.

Other people that I want to thank are the individuals from the University of Michigan-Dearborn who made this opportunity run smoothly. Randy who works in the Student Activities Office, worked side by side with Angela Walker at United Way of Southeastern Michigan on getting all the volunteers on board. We received emails and phone calls everyday to make sure we were updated with information on what was going on prior to our experience. Also to Regine Williams, who informed me about this event and insisted that I take apart in it, I want to say thank you and thank you again.

Lastly, I want to thank the community of people supporting me in this event. To my friends and family that stayed in touch with me while I endured this great experience, I say thank you. To Kawthar, Ryan, Terry, Natalie, Kristen and Randy for being a family to me during this entire trip to the Gulf Coast, I want to say thank you for your kind generosity and friendship that you displayed to me during my first flight and experience in Louisiana. You are individuals who I know will be very successful in life. So continue to keep your head high because your destination is influenced by your determination. To everyone else who may feel left out of this journal, I appreciate you following my experience and reading my journals. Again Thank You All!

3
After the Journey

We ourselves feel that what we are doing is just a drop in the ocean, but the ocean would be less because of that missing drop. We can do no great things, only small things with great love.

–Mother Theresa

This chapter chronicles the journals that I wrote for United Way for Southeastern Michigan to show the camaraderie that the local participants had after sharing Alternative Spring Break together. Again, I would like to emphasize that the group of students that participated in ASB 2007 from Michigan did not know each other before the experience. However as we shared such a wonderful, transformative experience together, it brought us closer together as friends and no one can ever take that away.

When we got back to Michigan after our experience, we began to reflect upon ASB. We went out and had lunch together at a local restaurant, where we ate and learned more about one another individually. We also did a service project with Habitat for Humanity Restore, where we reenacted our ASB experience and the time we shared. We would constantly contact one another to talk about our feelings and ways to bring the same ASB energy back to metropolitan Detroit. This sense of unity was important to us because we wanted to brainstorm ways we could be leaders in our own communities. Also no one else seemed to understand why our experience was so significant except for us.

I also would like to point out that United Way for Southeastern Michigan did a great job with keeping the group together and motivated as well. One night we went to a Pistons game, where we were recognized on court for our services. We also had a meeting with United Way staff on our campus to talk about our highs and lows during ASB. Lastly, we were even given the opportunity to meet with Michael Brennan, CEO of United Way for Southeastern Michigan, to talk about our efforts in Lake Charles, Louisiana.

Having this opportunity to socialize and share our thoughts on our experience made us feel that we had really made a difference. It also gave us a sense of empowerment that we are capable of making significant change in the region of southeastern Michigan. That week was very powerful and my life has never been the same. I realize that I am the difference that I want to see in my community and I can stand up for change when change is needed. So take the time to read my thoughts on ASB after I had settled in from such a great week of service in Lake Charles, Louisiana.

Sunday, March 25, 2007
Still Breadth-taking after One Week

It's been a week since ASB 2007 and "The Michigan Crew" can't stop talking about it. Throughout the week, we have reflected upon the amazing experience. Many people have continued to ask us how our trip was and we find that we can't put our reflections into words. Even as we continue to approach many interviews by the media, it is still difficult to explain the nature of this experience.

Much love goes out to United Way for being so organized during this event. They made sure that every team was leaving the Volunteer Housing Center at 8 a.m. every morning on their way to their project site. This level of organization made you respect the event a lot because it was clear that United Way was giving their best, so you had to do the same. Then each team worked on different projects, so when we came back to the Volunteer Housing Center, each group had different experiences to share. Also at the end of the volunteer day, all the students were able to mingle together and get to know each other and learn about each other's lives.

Tuesday, April 9, 2007
We're Here and Not Leaving
4/9/07

I'm back and I wanted to let everyone know about the "Michigan Crew" sticking together. Since we have been back, we have continued the open channels of communication among each other. This past Saturday we met to have dinner at 5 p.m. Randy and Natalie spoiled the party by not coming, but everyone else still had a blast being together. We reflected upon the good times of ASB and we continued to learn more and more about one another.

Also this past Thursday, we had a meeting with United Way of Southeastern Michigan, to discuss the highs and lows of the

ASB experience. We also discussed how we can continue our involvement in the community locally.

I was really excited because I got a chance to announce the new organization that I would be starting on campus next year. At the moment it is a secret until I get it established, but I will update those who are interested. United Way was happy to hear that we are still excited to continue our involvement locally and that we would be able to work with them to set up projects for next year.

So we are still here and we're not going anywhere. We are committed to the idea of social change through community involvement and we hope we can see you engaged with us in the future. May God Bless you and Happy Easter!

4

My Empowerment

Everybody can be great. Because everybody can serve. You don't have to have a college degree to serve. You don't have to make your subject and your verb agree to serve. You don't have to know about Plato and Aristotle to serve. You don't have to know Einstein's theory of relativity to serve. You don't have to know the second theory of thermodynamics in physics to serve. You only need a heart full of grace. A soul generated by love.

-Dr. Martin Luther King Jr.

When the local Michigan participants were given the opportunity to meet with Michael Brennan, the CEO of United Way for Southeastern Michigan, I was surprised because I didn't realize that our efforts were important enough to warrant meeting the President of our local United Way. As we sat down at the long table located on the 13th floor of 1212 Griswold in downtown Detroit, we began to talk about the wonderful experience that we had. In this meeting I was joined by Ryan Schreiber, Kristen Lewis and Randy Dillard from the University of Michigan-Dearborn, as well as other United Way for Southeastern Michigan staff.

When it was my turn to speak, I began to explain how Alternative Spring Break was a total transformative experience for me. I mentioned to Michael Brennan that I was in contact with my Mom throughout the week so that she would be updated on my status away from home. However, the comment that seemed to make the biggest difference to the room was when I mentioned that I was giving up basketball at my university to be more engaged in community service during my senior year. I also mentioned how I admired the civil rights era and the work of civil rights leader Dr. Martin Luther King, Jr., and what he did during that time period. I mentioned this movement because I realized that our nation is approaching a vital moment where change is needed, and I believe that my generation realizes and understands this and wants to be of service in any way possible.

After I shared my story and the meeting was finally over, Michael Brennan handed me his card and asked me to write up an essay on my experience and to send it to him by email. He told me that he was inspired by my words and actions to help the area of Lake Charles, Louisiana, and he felt that my story could inspire others.

In this chapter you will find the "Power of One" which was written by Michael Brennan, and his thoughts about what I said in the meeting. Secondly, you will find the essay that I wrote to Michael Brennan entitled, "I Matter in Making a Difference." Take your time to read through both of them because having the President of the local United Way write kind words about me, left me inspired and empowered to do more for the community, and to do everything at the best of my ability. From that day forward, I continued my involvement with United Way, and I began to inspire other students to become involved in the community as well.

Thursday, June 07, 2007
"Power of One"
By: Michael Brennan

"I made the decision to quit the basketball team, so I could dedicate more of my life to service." As I listened to the story of Adam Harris, I couldn't help but feel the world was a better place because he was in it.

This high achieving student/ athlete attends University of Michigan – Dearborn and had recently returned from participating in United Way's Alternative Spring Break (ASB). Over 400 college students from across America went to the gulf coast for their spring break to help in the never-ending recovery.

I wanted to take some time with them to learn more about their experience and explore "What's next?"

About half way through our discussion, Adam began to tell his journey. He told me that on his i-pod he has most of Martin Luther King's speeches. From Adam's perspective, Martin Luther King's life, the vision he shared, and the depth of thinking he possessed were as defining as any great thinker/doer/leader the world has known.

When he was in the Gulf Coast volunteering, he kept calling his mom to talk with her about what he was experiencing. More importantly, Adam was listening to what the voice deep inside of him was saying. He realized that while he loved basketball, the time required to do that well was something he no longer could do. He wanted to see that significant amount of time dedicated to service. To others. To community.

This is a man who at a very early age has his compass set on a true north. The power, strength and courage of his decision to dedicate his life to service will be felt by many. His example provides a teachable moment for others.

How will we make progress in this region? Through decisions like Adam's. The Power of One.

Wednesday, July 11, 2007
"I Matter in Making a Difference"

"I recently received a note from a young man who wrote a brief essay titled "I Matter in Making a Difference." When you wonder about the generation coming along, read this essay by Adam Harris to elevate your hope about the future."

– **Michael Brennan**

I Matter in Making a Difference
By: Adam Harris

Everyday I wake up I feel that I have a new reason to live. This reason to live has not evolved because it never existed, but it seems that there is a new spark that initiates this reason. This reason to live is not because I didn't love life, but it seems to give life more meaning. This reason to live has to do with the motivation and determination to make a difference. This reason to live has been sparked by the understanding that "I can and will make a difference."

My mother once told me that "hope deferred is long-suffering." This suffering can consist of hardships, a difficult phase of life, a problem in a relationship or even being submissive to the storms of life. It can even lead to life looking weary or a journey seeming fuzzy, but when one can realize that he/she faces this psychological condemnation, one can make an attempt to exit and overcome.

Being a 20 year-old African-American male attending The University of Michigan-Dearborn, I thought life finally made sense and there was nothing more to add. I figured I would receive my degree, choose a career and make a living for myself. Little did I know that one experience such as Alternative Spring Break through United Way for Southeastern Michigan and United Way of America would change my perspective on life.

This experience helped me realize the importance of giving back and the obligation that each member of society has to their community. It helped me understand that change can happen even on an individual level, but even greater on a collective level, when people work together. It opened my mind to see that everyone has his/her own talents and skills, and once everyone comes together to make a difference, change will occur.

So you might ask yourself, what matters in making a difference? I've come to understand that I matter, you matter and together we all matter in making a difference. United Way for Southeastern Michigan has shown me that my individual effort in Lake Charles, Louisiana, mattered in making a difference. I now understand that I no longer have to wait for a community service initiative to carry out my obligation to my community. I now understand that I don't have to wait until Spring Break comes back around to be involved and engaged in an alternative to make a difference. Lastly, I now understand that time continues to move, and if I want to make a change, I must start now.

With this new reason to live, I no longer have to hope for change but have faith in change. By definition, faith is a belief that does not rest on logical proof or material evidence. I like to think of faith as the belief to sit in a chair, knowing that chair will hold and support your weight, despite your body mass or weight. So with this faith, I've internalized consciously that I will make a difference and I do matter in mobilizing change. Martin Luther King, Jr., said; "This faith can give us courage to face the uncertainties of the future. It will give our tired feet new strength as we continue our forward stride toward the city of freedom."

So even though I do not know what tomorrow has in store, I do know that I will play a part in making a difference. We must move forward knowing that we are the advocates for change and our destination rests upon our decisions. We have the power to break away from the psychological condemnation that holds us down, and the ability to preserve our community within. Alternative Spring Break 2007 has shown me this new vision and I will use that experience to foster my new reason to live.

To view these blogs by Michael Brennan or other blogs by United Way for Southeastern Michigan, please visit: http://unitedwaysem.blogspot.com/

5
A Friend's Perspective

We make a living by what we get, but we make a life by what we give.
*-***Winston Churchill**

So often we can forget how much of an influence we have on others, and how our personal testimonies can activate the growth process or response within them. When I returned to Southeastern Michigan from Southwest Louisiana, I began to share with friends and others about my experience. I spoke to many groups on campus about the importance of volunteering and service in the community, while also explaining the importance of finding one's passion.

One of the friends that I had an opportunity to share my experience with was Tammy Russell. Tammy was a young lady that I met early on in my undergraduate years at the university because she played basketball for the women's team; just as I had played for the men's team at University of Michigan-Dearborn. Tammy and I became close friends through our encounters throughout our years playing, and she always had a good spirit and smile to share. As our friendship grew over the years, Tammy and I worked together in basketball camps hosted by the men's and women's teams throughout the summer. Because of the passion that I had for children and the game of basketball, Tammy, as well as other students, would help me to organize a camp experience that was fun and exciting for kids.

I noticed that over those years, I had a personal connection with Tammy that allowed me to be honest about my thoughts and feelings toward the university and my experiences in life. We would find moments to talk and share our ups and downs about things that were on our mind. Well, when I got back on campus I made sure to tell Tammy about my experience in Louisiana. She took time out of her day to allow me to go on and on about how this experience away from home changed my life. I also explained how it had transformed me so much that I was thinking about quitting basketball my senior year to be more involved in campus engagement and community service events.

A year later, our campus in partnership with United Way for Southeastern Michigan hosted an Alternative Spring Break in Metropolitan Detroit to work with local community agencies to help with the basic needs of the community. Tammy was a participant of this Alternative Spring Break Detroit experience in 2008. On the last day of the experience, Tammy rushed up to me after the day was over with tears in her eyes and said, "Adam, I need a hug." I immediately embraced her; and at that moment I began to understand that she was having a transformative experience, just as I had the previous year. Both of us decided to go into the volunteer office, located on the second floor of the University Center where we had many talks before, to talk about her experience that week. As Tammy was finally able to moderate her tears and gather her emotions, we began to talk about the week of ASB coming to a close.

Tammy began to explain to me that she had met a young lady who was just like her at Vista Maria. Vista Maria was one of the local community agencies that partnered with United Way during the ASB experience. This young lady was talented, motivated and had a dream to one day play college basketball. Tammy told me that she had realized how blessed and fortunate she was to have already accomplished that feat. As I began to listen even more with tears forming in her eyes, I realized that her tears were powered by her own testimony that she needed to share with me. Her testimony that she wanted me to hear was that she wanted to continue mentoring that young lady even after Alternative Spring Break was over. Well as of this day, I am grateful to say and pleased with Tammy because she continued her mentoring responsibilities where she was able to help the young lady graduate from high school.

It is truly stories such as Tammy's that seem to come out of the Alternative Spring Break experience because she not only gave of herself, but she also gave of her heart. From this day forward, we will never be able to measure the impact that Tammy had on the young lady, neither will we be able to measure the impact that the young lady will have on her own community. It is decisions like these that make life so beautiful to share with one another, and I am happy that I shared ASB Detroit with Tammy and other dedicated students.

Sometimes life gives us a choice, and our ability to make a decision is the opportunity at hand. We can either decide to act or not to act, but the decision is ours. Tammy made the decision to act and continue her involvement with making a difference in this young lady's life. Because of Tammy's commitment and purpose to help, a young lady found a new sense of meaning for her life. She was encouraged when she was low in spirit; she was inspired when times seemed hopeless, and saw the dawning of a new day through her dark nights of sorrow. Tammy made a difference and encouraged a young lady to make a change in her life.

I asked Tammy if she could write up her thoughts on me after I returned from my trip to Lake Charles, Louisiana. I felt it was important to give you a different perspective because as I came back I wanted to share my excitement with others, and she was one person that I had to listen. Her testimony and tears reminds me of my experience and I am thankful for her kind words.

"Over the course of a lifetime, we come across individuals from different walks of life. Each unique soul that we stumble upon touches our inner self in their own special and significant ways. There are those who make subtle impacts, and those who have been there for longer than we can remember; the latter of the two are those we trust wholeheartedly, and are there to guide us through life's well beaten path. While each individual makes his/her own noteworthy impact, the lucky few are able to find a special person that positively influences their life, and aids in awakening the person within themselves that they never knew existed. That exceptional person in my life, that I have been fortunate enough to befriend, is Adam Harris.

I first met Adam in 2004, while playing basketball for the University of Michigan-Dearborn. He was always the modest type, who consistently remained focused and worked diligently on every task at hand. His views on life and his work ethics were always inspiring to anyone who interacted with Adam and willingly reached out to him. It wasn't until our college spring break in 2007 that I was able to realize what absolutely made Adam Harris such a distinctive person. Rather than taking off to the typical spring break "hot spots," Adam admirably embarked on a journey with United Way's Alternative Spring Break (ASB) program to the Gulf Coast, where he dedicated his time and energy to the hurricane relief effort in Lake Charles, Louisiana.

Spring break had come to an end, and upon our return to campus it was evident that a spark had ignited within Adam, a small spark of passion for unselfishly making a difference in the lives of those less fortunate than he. Throughout the year, Adam and I would reminisce about his adventures along the Gulf Coast. Adam's ASB experience had equipped him with the proper tools to embark on his own philanthropic journey, and it wasn't long before he took his experiences in Louisiana and applied them in his own community. Adam's outlook of ASB was always so positive, that I could feel his enthusiasm and eagerness to continue his voyage. I couldn't help but be intrigued by every breath and picture he had to share about his ASB experience, that in the summer of 2007, when Adam asked me to join him in his efforts to enhance community involvement through Students Working Onward Together (SWOT), I respectfully took on the role as Business Relations Representative. Adam worked diligently to brainstorm and construct his student organization, which is continuously growing and continuing to serve the community.

I wish that I could describe to all of you the immense generosity and humbleness that is Adam Harris, a man who is selfless and compassionate in his endeavors. Helen Keller once made a statement that reinforces Adam's chosen destiny. She said: "Happiness cannot come from without. It must come from within...first for the other fellow and then for ourselves." Adam has always, and continues to put others and their well being before his own. He was fortunate enough to apply his experiences in Louisiana to his everyday life here in Michigan. He continues to strive for excellence to assure that he touches the lives of all those he encounters. Adam's work is never complete, as he is diligently working to make society a more happy and enjoyable place to call home!"

-**Tammy Russell**

Students Working Onward Together at ASB Detroit
Back Row (left to right): Britta Roan, Dewnya Bakri, Tammy Russell, Adam Harris, and Danny Kimmel. Middle (kneeling): Leticia Horry.

6
What did I learn?

> *The magnitude of our social problems will require that all citizens and institutions make a commitment to volunteering as a way of life and as a primary opportunity to create needed change.*
>
> **-George Romney**

I believe that there is a time in our lives where we become unselfishly more concerned about the well being of another than the well being of ourselves. For some people this psychological understanding can blossom early on in one's life or it can surface in the latter years of an individual. We all have moments in our lives where we pull together and remind ourselves of the importance of family and community. It is filled in the spirit of the holidays and gains momentum for those we love and cherish.

A true example of this care for another can be seen in the eyes of a father as he looks forward to being the protector and provider of his children. For the mother it can be immediately recognized during the birth of a child, as she embraces the baby with a comforting cradle in her arms. This care for another soul speaks to the spirit of giving from the heart and embodies the love that we have for one another.

In some cultures, the concept of "Charity starts at home" is practiced, which simply means that kind generosity and goodwill begins with one's own family and community. With this belief, a person is expected to enrich the value of his own community before he extends a handout to the larger community. It is simply put in place to remind individuals of the place from which they've come from and to never forget that one has an obligation to give back to their own community.

In my experience with the Alternative Spring Break, I never imagined that I would see a group of young college students with so much excitement and energy in an effort to give back. This effort was far beyond giving back to one's own community. It reached into the lives and hearts of those recovering from disaster. It even helped me realize why I must continue to give back and the importance for this decision to be a life-long determination.

One thing that I learned while being on this journey of service near the Gulf coast is that people love to give back and participate in being caring citizens of not only their own communities but of communities around the world. The Vice Chancellor of Enrollment Management and Student Life at the University of Michigan-Dearborn has a well-known speech on community. He refers to our university as a "Community of Higher Education" instead of an institution of higher education. When he begins to explain this concept, he mentions that in a community you must be an active participant and not just receive the benefits of being a part of that community. He then goes on to show an example by welcoming everyone with a greeting such as, "Good evening!" Now according to his definition of community, if you do not participate in greeting him back with the same energy that he exerted, then you are not being a true participant in the university's "Community of Higher Education."

I also learned that being involved within your community will help you begin to understand the true problems and underlying issues that your community might be facing. How can we expect to solve the problems of homelessness, hunger, foreclosure, violence or high school dropout if we have never been exposed to those problems or participated in an experience that gives us an up close and personal look at them? Earlier this year I went to a national student Impact Conference in Boston, Massachusetts. I attended a session called "Faces of Homelessness." At this session, which had probably more than 200 college students from all across the country present, the audience was moved by the personal testimonies of individuals who were homeless.

I remember listening to a young girl who was the daughter of a middle-aged mother who was put out on the streets to live. As the young girl, probably around the age of 12 began to tell her story, I remember her saying: "Don't judge people who are homeless before you even know their story or why they are homeless." After her speech, she received a standing ovation for her boldness in speaking out and telling her story. She was also given many compliments on how well she was able to speak given her youth. I personally was so moved by her story that I stood up and asked her to sign the book that I received from the national conference because she had motivated me to new heights to continue the work that I do in the community. She willingly signed my book, and I will never forget how intelligent she was and her understanding of the importance of not judging others.

I mentioned that experience to say that the answer to the problems of our communities around the country exists in the heart of those communities. At times we think we understand the issues that local communities are facing, but we really don't. I truly believe that if we want to change our society, and make change that is sustainable and measurable, we must see that change coming from within those communities. Instead of throwing money at the problem or suggesting a solution for the problem, the best answer would be to collaborate with people in those communities to find solutions to their own problems.

One last experience that I will share with you comes from an encounter that I had with local high school students at Southwestern High School in Detroit. The students were trying to raise money to take a trip to Malawi, Africa, and they were planning a dinner to raise money. The group was planning to have an auction of black and white photos that would be enlarged and put on easels. I remember one young lady suggested to the supervisor of the group that she could use a computer program to color one individual thing within the picture, to bring out that part of the photo.

At that very moment I saw how creative the youth still are within the city of Detroit. Sometimes it is little suggestions like those that work toward the construction and empowerment of our children across the nation. She had a photo of her friends near a train track and she wanted to bring out one of the lights on the pole on the train tracks in the photo. I will never forget that suggestion for as long as I live because one of two things could have happened. The supervisor could have supported the suggestion, making the young lady feel significant and empowered or she could have shot down the suggestion, making her suggestion feel unimportant and not significant at all. That day I was happy to see that the supervisor supported the suggestion, and the young girl walked away feeling empowered that she had suggested a great idea.

So as I think about Alternative Spring Break Detroit in 2008, I saw a dream that could have been supported or left unrealized. Alternative Spring Break Detroit was birthed out of the same experience that I had in Lake Charles, Louisiana in 2007. During my experience and the phone conversation that I had with my Mom on the last day, I realized that Detroit needed just as much help in some areas just as Louisiana was recovering from Hurricane Rita. So in our meeting with the local United Way for Southeastern Michigan, I mentioned how important it was that I helped to get more students involved in service events throughout southeastern Michigan. I mentioned that bringing an experience to Detroit, such as Alternative Spring Break could really help revitalize an urban community trying to get back on its feet.

So this is why I am so gracious and thankful to United Way for believing in my dream to bring an experience to the city of Detroit for students to participate in. When I left ASB 2007, I felt empowered to make a difference. Going into my senior year, I knew it was a year of great things but I couldn't quite tell what would happen. Going back to the journals and write-ups, I felt empowered but humble that Michael Brennan would write about my decision to quit basketball and dedicate more of my time to service in the local community. He really inspired me and gave me full support for a dream and idea (ASB Detroit), that has now changed my life and the lives of others.

It is my hope that you can learn from my example and the example of the other students who participated in ASB 2007 of how important it is to be involved in your local community. Whether your involvement is with United Way, Boys and Girls Club of America, Americorps, your local church, or initiating your own community event, I hope you can see how significant it is for you to be involved. Don't be the person who sits quietly knowing that you have a possible solution, but be engaged in every possible way you can. As the Vice Chancellor of Enrollment Management and Student Life at the University of Michigan-Dearborn would say, "Be an active participant in your community." Just remember, it is your duty, your responsibility and freedom that this beautiful country called America gives you. You are the change that you want to see in your community, and I guarantee you that by your example, you will immediately inspire and empower those around you.

The Last Day of Alternative Spring Break Detroit 2008

What do you need to serve?

It's simple! Dr. Martin Luther King Jr., said it best: "You only need a heart full of grace. A soul generated by love."

EMPATHY. LOVE. COMPASSION.
(ELC)

7
How you can get Involved

Our deepest fear is not that we are inadequate. Our deepest fear is that we are powerful beyond measure.

– **Marianne Williamson**

When reading about my journey in the Gulf Coast region of Southwest Louisiana, you may have asked yourself the question, "What is Adam's advice on getting involved?" I have three words for you: FIND YOUR PASSION! Passion is any powerful or compelling emotion or feeling, such as love or hate (*Dictionary.com*). What this simply means is either you love what you do or you dislike it. You either enjoy what you do or you do not. It sets the premise that you can not straddle the fence with your passion because you would only be fooling yourself.

My passion deals with sports. The one sport that I seem to love the most is basketball. What I enjoy the most while analyzing the game or being a spectator of the game is how players on the floor impact the game in their own significant way. Whether you are big or small, it doesn't seem to matter if you ask a person do they enjoy the game.

Whether I am watching the game or actually playing the game, I always make a conscious decision to be a student of the game. When I was young child growing up, my ultimate dream was to be good enough to play basketball at the collegiate level. I was always smaller than the normal kid at my grade level, so I knew that it was not my destiny to play basketball professionally. To help you understand how small I was, I entered the ninth grade at 4 feet 11 inches tall (maybe 5 feet with my shoes on).

As I began to mature into a young man and as a dedicated student of the game, I made a promise to myself that I would one day begin to teach the game to others as my way of giving back. As so many players and coaches have given of their time to teach me the game of basketball, I saw the significance and impact that each individual left upon my life. It was during those moments that I began to realize that it is the competitive spirit that athletes have that should allow them to be leaders in their classrooms and leaders in their communities. Sports teams have always given schools and communities something to rally behind, which in return has many children looking up to local athletes and those who play at the professional level.

Every summer I get involved with basketball camps. In my neighborhood there are unlimited opportunities for individuals to give a little bit of their time to volunteer. I choose to be involved with local sports organizations in my community to help young children become better basketball players. Seeing smiles on the faces of the children when they are motivated to keep trying, encouraged to keep shooting, or comforted at their lowest moments, helps me to know that I am making a difference in their lives. So in return I feel good, the children feel good, and the families enjoy watching their children having a good time. In the end, everyone is rewarded.

My passion to help children learn the game of basketball starts when I wake up and I realize that that day I will help a child learn the fundamentals of basketball. I say my prayers, meditate and make sure I am in good spirits to help the child or children that I will be working with. Secondly, I go over in my mind everything I want them to learn and understand about the game. Lastly, I want them to have fun. This game will only allow so many to make it to the professional level; however, there are skills that can be transferred into other areas of life such as teamwork, dedication, practice, and hard work.

As I enter the gym involved with a camp or to help a child become a better basketball player, I try to set the tone by saying, "I am here to help you but I want you to have fun." It is important for children to enjoy the game at an early age so that it doesn't feel like they're being forced to play the game. As I begin to teach the fundamentals of the game, I lead by example by showing the child how to perform the necessary drill or game at hand. During this time I begin to notice a lot of mentoring happening between myself and the player because depending on the work ethic of the child, it can determine the limit of how far you can push the child to be the best they can be.

Some of the mentoring that I notice is reassuring the child that he/she can complete the task at hand. "I can't do it! (Whining)," the child would say. Then I would have to tell the child, "Yes you can, just try it again." When I was raised as child "can't" was not in my vocabulary, and I could not say this at home or around my parents. This lesson of encouragement is so important because if the child is allowed to discredit themselves in believing that they can not accomplish a task, it will carry over into other aspects of life. Always remember that your mindset can manifest your destiny and your future is unlimited to endless possibilities.

As the session of coaching would come to a close, I would remind the child of the skills and lessons that I taught him/her. Important lessons that I stress are believing in who you are, the importance of practice, and hard work. A child must recognize that he/she will never accomplish a task if he/she does not believe in themself. Secondly, I was always told as a young player that practice doesn't make perfect but a perfect practice does. This simply means to make the necessary adjustments to do what is right the next time after you have learned from your mistakes. Lastly, I always encourage a child to work hard and to be their best when they step on the floor because hard work allows you to make up for other areas that you may not be as skillful in.

At the end of the day, I begin to evaluate and ask myself, "What could I have done better?" My passion constantly has me questioning myself, "How can I make it better next time?" It sometimes keeps me up at night wondering whether I pushed the child to be the best that they can be. I even have dreams, and at times I wake up in the middle of the night in realization of what I could possibly try out the next time.

Your passion should allow you to exert a ton of energy without you realizing it because it's that compelling and strong desire you have to do what you are trying to accomplish. When I work with children, my energy level is through the roof because I love instructing them to become better basketball players. However, I have also learned to control my emotions and energy because I realize that everyone is not always as passionate about teaching and learning the game of basketball like I am.

I mentioned in a few paragraphs above that everyone is rewarded if the person who is acting upon their passion is truly carrying it out. The reason for this is because you are doing something natural that is in your God given ability, and you are displaying an aspect of your life that God has blessed you with called talent. Talent is a special natural ability or aptitude (*Dictionary.com*). You can begin to find your gift and talent in times where you are pressured and forced to perform under certain situations. You will notice that you are calm and collected, while everyone else may be frightened or uncertain of what to do.

Some examples of talent being on display are professional athletes like Michael Jordan and Tiger Woods. Whether or not you enjoy watching these two professional athletes in their respective sports, it is evident that they are two of the most gifted athletes in the history of sports. One way you can tell that they have a gift is because they remain calm in pressure situations. For Michael Jordan, he is the one player who actually wants the ball when the game is on the line and the team is down one or two points. He understands that the defense is at his mercy, and to win or lose the game will be decided by his confidence to take the shot in that particular situation. When Tiger Woods performs on the golf course, he treats every shot the same by staying poised and in the moment. He doesn't allow the golf course to throw him off, and he makes the necessary adjustments to the next shot. The truth is there are talented people all around you because they understand their strengths and weaknesses.

Could you imagine if Martin Luther King Jr. was never a minister? What if Michael Jordan was never a basketball player? How about if Michelangelo was never a painter? Or if the beautiful words of Maya Angelou were never spoken? What if Barack Obama, who is living the true American Dream, never ran for president? What I am saying is we are all born with gifts and talents that make us the unique individuals that we are. It is the reason that some of us use the right side of our brain and others of us use the left side. It is the reason some of us are motivated to take the initiative while others stand silent and keep a watchful eye. It is also the very reason that some of us are even considered leaders, and others maybe considered team players or adherents. However don't rain on your own parade if you're considered an adherent, silent or left brained because even the greatest people of our time had weaknesses. Also it is the only way our society can truly operate, that is when others are in tune with who they are.

Let me give you an example. I mentioned Michael Jordan above, and I enjoyed watching him play basketball during his career, but when he decided to quit basketball to play baseball, he served himself a nightmare. Even with all the hype of him going to baseball, his hard work and dedication just couldn't transfer over to make him the baseball player that he was in basketball. However as you noticed when Michael Jordan decided to return to the game of basketball he won three more titles with the Chicago Bulls. So as you can see, basketball was his strength and baseball was one of his weaknesses; at least at the professional level.

So the message that I am trying to build in your conscious is to be the best that you can be. God has blessed us all with talents and gifts that we can liberate ourselves from frustration, and liberate others by our own example. In the Drum Major Instinct, Martin Luther King Jr., said: "I want you to say that I tried to love and serve humanity." Well Dr. King did just that with the talents God gave him. He went all across the world preaching non-violence and supporting grass root organizations such as the Student Nonviolent Coordinating Committee (SNCC). He also realized that the civil rights movement was not just a fight for equality in the United States but was also a quest for equal opportunities across the world. His position on being against the war in Vietnam speaks to his compassion for humanity and the equality of all mankind. Dr. King gave his life, his gift and talent to humanity, and it is because of God fearing men like him that others can be service to their own community.

    I believe that everyone has a part to play in the social construction of life. Finding your passion will help you to enjoy life and to not burden yourself with its worries. We all have something to offer our communities and there is no better gift that we can give than the time we share getting involved.

The Ultimate Goal

Inspired and written for servants all across the world.

If I can open my mouth
And let the truth be told,

If I can pray for the sick
Or inspire a soul,

If I can take what's broken
And with God's power make it whole,

Then I will be living within the expression
The true ultimate goal.

The vision is worth the dream.
Each step is worth the journey.
His purpose is worth my destiny.

A True Heart to Give: Gloria House

Thank you from the depths of my heart, for the freedom of my conscious mind and for the rivers of opportunity you provided me. You gave life to a new generation; that generation is me.

-**Adam Harris**

This section of *A Heart to Give* gives me the opportunity to present to you my mentor and close friend, Dr. Gloria House. Dr.

House is the former Director of the African and African American studies department at the University of Michigan-Dearborn. In my first semester at the university, I had an African American Literature class with Dr. House. What amazed me the most about my friend and close confidant during that class was the humble spirit and modesty that she possessed.

When I learned about the significant role that Dr. House played in the Civil Rights Movement, it blew my mind to know that she never mentioned it. I learned of her involvement in the Student Nonviolent Coordinating Committee (SNCC), in which hundreds of students (college students) gave up their lives for the opportunities that I have today. She worked constantly during her time as an activist holding registration drives for people to register to vote. I also realize how blessed I am to have graduated from the University of Michigan-Dearborn, an higher educational institution like many others where African Americans were not always allowed to have the access or opportunity to apply. It is because of this that I am thankful to the people who fought for justice and equality, not just in the US but also around the world.

Dr. House is an amazing mentor to many students at the university including myself. I titled this section "A True Heart to Give" because even with all her accomplishments as a social activist during the late 60's and early 70's, Dr. House continues to fight for justice and equal opportunities for youth and young adults across Metropolitan Detroit. Her work goes beyond the classroom and into writing poetry and editing this book that you have in your hands. Dr. House also serves on the Board of Directors for Broadside Press in Detroit as the Vice President. She is affiliated with other great activist organizations, and she is a true leader for African Americans on the campus at the University of Michigan-Dearborn.

It gives me great pleasure and honor to write about Dr. Gloria House in this book because her life resembles the true essence of A Heart to Give. You can always find her office open for a friendly visit, or you can see her casually walking around campus with a beautiful smile. Her phone call to remind me of my gift to write and the ability to communicate with others allowed me to be encouraged to write this book, and it will never be forgotten. I thank God that our paths have crossed because she is a great servant to humanity. God bless you Dr. House and thank you for all that you have done and all that you continue to do!

About the Author

One is not born into the world to do everything but to do something.
-Henry David Thoreau

Adam Harris grew up in Southfield, Michigan his entire life. He went to Southfield Public Schools until the middle of his ninth grade year. He then transferred to Royal Oak Public Schools for the duration of his high school career, and graduated from Royal Oak Dondero High School. Upon graduation, Adam applied to University of Michigan-Dearborn, where he was accepted to major in Business Administration and minor in African and African American Studies.

Some of Adam's accomplishments while being in college were playing on the Men's Varsity Basketball team for two years, and red shirting his freshman year. His senior year was the biggest turn of events because Adam decided to forgo his senior basketball season to be immersed in community service events. At the end of his senior year, Adam was awarded the University's Distinguished Student Leader Award. Adam also received the Heart and Soul Award from Michigan Campus Compact, and was recognized by United Way for the United Way Young Adult Award of Excellence. Adam's efforts even reached state-wide recognition by becoming a finalist for the Governor's Service Awards under the category of Youth Volunteer of the Year.

Currently, Adam is working on his Master's degree in Community Counseling at the University of Detroit Mercy. He understands that continuing his education will only help him to serve his community better and more efficient in the days ahead. And with a forecast of his future of the next 10 years, Adam hopes to have graduated with a PhD in African American Studies.

Adam is very humbled that he has finally written his first book. He says that this is the first of many that he will write. Adam has made sure to thank all of his mentors and family for all of their support in the process.

Graduation Day, April 2008

Now is the time for you to make a difference. How will you make a difference in your community?

My Prayer Today

It is my prayer today that you found hope, strength, and inspiration within the pages of this book. My story that you now have is not just a testament to me and my willingness to serve but a testament to students and individuals all across the country that are making a difference. I hope that you realize the potential that you have inside of you to mark this journey of life, and your ability to influence the lives of others. May God bless you now and in your future of making a difference in your community!

NOTES

NOTES

NOTES

NOTES

NOTES

NOTES

NOTES